ISAAC NEWTON

A Life From Beginning to End

Copyright © 2017 by Hourly History

Table of Contents

Introduction

If ever there was a man who believed he was on par with God, it was Sir Isaac Newton. Coming from humble beginnings and moving through the ranks of the science of his day, Newton became a darling of the scientific world. In fact, he changed the way we understand the universe.

Isaac Newton was the man who discovered the laws of gravity and motion, and along with that, he delved deep into mathematics, creating calculus. The worldview of most twenty-first-century inhabitants stems from how his discoveries helped to shape the world.

Yet, his world was a shambles. Born early and unwanted by either father or mother, he would eventually head off into the solitude that he craved and loved so much; and when confronted would argue bitterly with anyone who stood in his way. Working in secrecy, often imposing long periods of isolation upon himself, Newton discovered and achieved more things than one would think humanly possible.

Newton laid the foundation for the world in which we live today. Theoretical and applied science owes its thanks to Sir Isaac Newton for carving the paths down which he so arrogantly strode. Because of the scientific breakthroughs he had, other esteemed scientists, such as Nikola Tesla and Thomas Edison, were able to complete the work that lay before them. Without Newton, none of that would have happened.

Isaac Newton was a wonder of his day and age. He had the ability to look at complex concepts of light and motion; he discovered what gravity is all about, he explained the universe, and gave to humanity its one and rightful place in the vast cosmos.

Come along then, for a journey into the mind and life of Isaac Newton. See how he encouraged debate among his peers and looked into the face of uncertainty with hope. There was always a challenge to behold. Newton was, and is, regarded as the chief architect of the modern world. Find out why in this book.

Chapter One

The English Civil War

"Men build too many walls and not enough bridges."

—Isaac Newton

Before getting into how Isaac Newton influenced the world, it's a good idea to take a look at the world in which he was born. When Queen Elizabeth I had died in 1603, the crown transferred to her cousin James, who was already king of Scotland. He then became King James I of England. He ruled, relatively peacefully until 1625, when he was succeeded by his son Charles I. Charles wanted to unite England, Scotland, and Ireland into one country. This didn't sit very well with those in Parliament. They believed England's traditions regarding the monarchy would be lost.

As things were at the time, Parliament played a minor role in English politics in the seventeenth century. They were summoned at the whim of the king and met only occasionally. They were almost what you might call an advisory committee to the ruler. Yet, the king couldn't ignore them, as he needed them to collect revenues throughout the land.

In order to do this, the gentry, who were a step up from the peasants, would elect representatives to sit in the

House of Commons. When they were assembled with the House of Lords, they formed the Parliament together. They really had no power to act on their own; they could only petition the king for bills they wished passed. If there was trouble, Parliament could threaten to withhold revenue.

Charles had married a Roman Catholic, which didn't sit well in Reformation England. To make matters worse, he got involved in an expeditionary force that went to France and resulted in a fiasco. At this point, Charles dissolved Parliament, and in 1628, he assembled a new one. One of the members of this new Parliament was Oliver Cromwell.

For the next ten years, Charles never called a Parliament. He ruled on his own, but with little money. Rather than do things the correct way by working with Parliament, Charles began imposing taxes for the most ridiculous things. More and more citizens were becoming enraged at his activities. Then, when religion started to get mixed into the equation, things began to take a turn for the worse.

Charles had appointed William Laud as Archbishop of Canterbury. The Puritans accused Laud of reintroducing Catholicism. The Roman Catholic religion had been forced underground or out of the country altogether under Elizabeth I, and there was widespread animosity towards anyone who followed Catholicism.

Puritans found themselves fined for not attending church and in continued hot water for opposing the king. In some cases, they were arrested. When Charles tried forcing his religious sanctions on Scotland, all hell broke loose. A rebellion ensued, but Charles agreed to stay out of Scottish religious affairs.

In 1640, Charles invaded Scotland anyway. Nothing was decisive, and the border was lined with English on one side and Scots on the other. The Scottish army had moved into England and demanded money not to burn and pillage the northern villages. This was a difficult request to accommodate as Charles himself was desperate for money.

Finally, in November 1640, Charles summoned the Long Parliament. They wanted to meet regularly, and there were to be no new taxes. Also, the king would no longer have the right to dissolve Parliament.

Alas, things grew worse, as the king kept opposing Parliament. In January 1642, Charles tried to have five members of the House of Commons arrested for treason. The attempt failed. So, he took his family out of London and made for a northern location. As the summer wore on, people were taking sides. Cities were all for Parliament, while the rural areas backed the king.

Little by little, tensions rose as more information surfaced. The king and his supporters were for the traditional government while the Parliamentarians supported everything from traditional government to redistribution of power at the national level. However, both sides seemed to favor having Charles I as king.

Forces gathered behind both factions, and by October 23, 1642, the first battle began. It was fought at Edgehill, and although neither side won, they both claimed victory.

In November the Battle of Turnham Green was fought, and Charles and his troops were forced to retreat to the city of Oxford. This would remain his base for the remainder of the war.

Suddenly, England seemed a place of confusion, darkness, and obscurity. Nothing was as it had once been. Faiths which had once ruled were gone, replaced by new beliefs and magic which was a great part of daily life. The plague was a daily concern, and many people believed the end of the world was near. England was learning to reshape itself, and it still had a long and bloody way to go.

It was on Christmas Day that very year that Isaac Newton was born. England was using the Julian calendar at the time, which meant that, technically, it was already January 4, 1643. His birth took place at Woolsthorpe, Lincolnshire, in a rural stone farmhouse.

His father, also named Isaac Newton, had died three months before the birth. The first Isaac Newton never learned to read or write and wrote his signature with an X. Woolsthorpe was near an ancient Roman road and children would occasionally unearth Roman coins in the dirt. Isaac's father was poor all of his life but did manage to have a comfortable farmer's existence.

Isaac Newton was born prematurely. He was such a tiny baby that his prospects looked bleak. His mother, Hannah Ayscough, unwillingly became a single mother. She didn't want her son, and thus, Isaac was raised by his maternal grandmother Margery Ayscough.

It seemed as if the infant Isaac was a child without a family. He certainly was a child without a country. England would soon broil over into civil war.

Chapter Two

Early Life

"Pick a flower on earth and you move the farthest star."

—Paul A.M. Dirac

By the time Isaac was three years old, his mother Hannah had remarried to the Reverend Barnabas Smith. She no longer had any time for Isaac. Hannah went on to have three children with the reverend; Isaac always maintained much animosity towards him and didn't think kindly of his mother either.

As a nineteen-year-old, Isaac had composed a list of sins. Some of his journals have been preserved, and one of the most interesting is this book of sins, published in 1662. Some of his sins included, "Using the word God openly, making pies on Sunday night, carelessly hearing and committing many sermons, having unclean thoughts, actions and dreams, punching my sister, not loving Thee for Thyself, and caring for worldly things more than God." Number thirteen was rather intriguing; "Threatening my father and mother Smith to burn them and the house over them." The young Isaac sounded like the typical teenager of his day.

As Isaac grew, more uprisings between the king and parliamentary forces were taking place. By the time Isaac was six, the Parliamentarians had put down most of the skirmishes in England. One of the leaders who stood against the king was Oliver Cromwell. He would successfully lead his men into battle time and time again.

By 1648, members of Parliament had had it with the king. They knew about his secret alliances and the way he was scheming to remain in power, and they were debating whether he should stay as king or not. Finally, in December 1648, the army marched on Parliament and arrested many of them. This "Rump Parliament" was told to bring charges of treason against the king. This allowed Oliver Cromwell to rise to power.

The king was found guilty of high treason. He was beheaded at the Palace of Whitehall on January 30, 1649. Isaac Newton was all of seven years old and a student at The King's School, in Grantham. By now England no longer had a king. Neither did they have a Parliament, only a Lord Protector, Oliver Cromwell. Royalists, including Charles' son, also named Charles, had fled to the island of Jersey off the English coast to wait out this rule called the Commonwealth. They would be there for some time.

While at school, Isaac loved his solitude. He sought solace in books. He didn't think much of literature or poetry but was deeply fascinated by mechanics and technology. He was taught Latin and Greek and also a solid foundation in mathematics.

By 1659, Isaac's mother had him returned to Woolsthorpe where she wanted him to be a farmer. Her second husband had died, and she needed Isaac to run the farm. He hated farming. The master of The King's School, Henry Stokes, pleaded with Hannah to have Isaac return. She relented, and Isaac came back to class, where he became the star student. He took a liking to building sundials and models of windmills.

While he was home, his mind never stopped conceiving. Newton recalled how he noticed how sunlight crept along the walls of his house. As the rays passed through the windows, they cast slanted edges. He observed how these slant edges shifted between sharp and bright images, revealing what looked to him to be a three-dimensional view.

Interested in what he was seeing, the young Newton began drawing sketches of circles and arches trying to measure time. He measured small distances with strings and was able to calculate inches into minutes in an hour.

At school, Newton kept to himself. Most other students socialized quite a bit, but he stuck to his books and did many chores to help pay for his schooling, as his mother gave him no money.

During this time, in the 1650s, England was without a ruler. Charles II had fled to his island of Jersey, and Oliver Cromwell continued small battles here and there. Cromwell was able to suppress the troops in Ireland where 3,500 people were massacred at the Battle of Drogheda. Ireland finally surrendered its troops to the English forces in 1653.

With the king's execution, Scotland had looked to Charles II to become their new ruler. Cromwell couldn't prevent Charles from marching into Scotland, then deep into England where he was defeated. He was able to escape to France. Political control was now through Parliament.

By 1658, Oliver Cromwell was dead. His son Richard became Lord Protector, but the Army didn't like him. Eventually, he was removed, and the Rump Parliament was in charge.

In April 1661, Charles II was restored to the throne of England. His coronation is known as The Restoration. In June that same year, Isaac Newton was admitted to Trinity College, Cambridge. His uncle, the Reverend William Ayscough, had also studied there. Newton paid his way by performing valet's duties, until 1664, when he was awarded a scholarship. This guaranteed him four more years until he could get his master's degree.

When Newton was at Trinity College, their teachings were based on those of Aristotle. Newton also supplemented his studies with learning about the philosophies of Descartes and Galileo. He kept a notebook known as Quaestiones all about mechanical philosophy. By 1665, Newton had discovered the general binomial theorem which led him to begin developing a mathematical theory which later became calculus.

During his years at Trinity College, Newton was influenced by the scientific and literary revolutions going on in Europe at the time. Copernicus and Kepler had already conceived their heliocentric view of the universe, and this would later be refined by Galileo.

It seemed that anywhere you looked in Europe during these years, new ideas were percolating. Not only were religious reformers coming along, but theories of many different kinds were, at last, seeing the light of day. Rene Descartes, for instance, had developed a theory in mechanical philosophy which stated that the mind and body are two distinct entities and that they co-exist. This approach would eventually grow into the "mind-body dualism."

Newton began viewing the world as one which is made up of a combination of bodies existing together in harmony. He then took it upon himself to study these various bodies. His studies were the beginnings of quantum physics.

Although the college was still teaching courses in a traditional way, Newton spent much of his free time reading the books of modern philosophers. Then in 1664, Trinity College hired a professor of mathematics; the first time ever in their history. His name was Isaac Barrow, and he was only nine years older than Newton. He had become the first occupant of the Lucasian chair at Cambridge.

Newton began attending his lectures and was drawn to his philosophies. By the end of the summer of 1665, Newton had obtained his bachelor's degree. The college was then shut for some time, due to the recrudescence of the plague. Newton returned home. Back in Woolsthorpe, he continued to enrich himself by learning all he could about such subjects as optics, calculus, and the theory of gravitation.

It was in his mother's garden that Newton had his famous epiphany about gravity. He watched an apple fall from a tree.

Chapter Three

Newton and the Apple

"Millions saw the apple fall, but Newton was the one who asked why."

—Bernard Baruch

It was while living at home in Woolsthorpe that something rather peculiar happened to Isaac Newton. Because the plague was once again making its rounds all over England, Trinity College was closed until the danger passed. So, Newton returned home and there engrossed himself in books.

Isaac took himself outside and was sitting under an apple tree when, suddenly, down comes an apple and hits him on the head. Instantly Newton understands that this force—gravity—which made the apple fall towards the Earth, is the same force that keeps the Moon and the stars from crashing into Earth.

Or maybe it didn't happen like that at all. Believe it or not, the apple didn't fall on Newton's head, and he didn't have an instant flash of inspiration about gravity at that moment. But, there is a truthful account of what ensued in the garden, which had been hidden away in the Royal Archives and revealed in 1752.

One William Stukeley recorded in his *Memoirs of Sir Isaac Newton's Life* a conversation he had with Newton in 1726.

"We went into the garden & drank thea under the shade of some appletrees, only he & myself, he told me, he was just in the same situation, as when formerly, the notion of gravitation came into his mind. 'Why should that apple always descend perpendicularly to the ground,' thought he to himself, occasioned by the fall of an apple, as he sat in a contemplative mood, 'why should it not go sideways or upwards? But constantly to the earth's center?' Assuredly the reason is, that the earth draws it, there must be a drawing power in matter & the sum of the drawing power in the matter of the earth must be in the earth's center, not in any side of the earth. Therefore, does this apple fall perpendicularly, or toward the center. If matter thus draws matter, it must be in proportion of its quantity. Therefore the apple draws the earth, as well as the earth draws the apple."

John Conduitt, Newton's assistant at the Royal Mint, also relayed the story that in the year 1666 while deep in thought and meandering around his mother's garden, Newton thought about an apple falling to the ground. The power of gravity was not limited to a certain distance from the earth, but this power must extend much further than was thought at the time. Newton speculated as to why the apple did not fall towards the Moon, and how, if the apple went into space, something would affect its orbit.

With these thoughts in mind, Newton began calculating what would be the end results of all his speculating. In the 1660s, Newton was tackling the issue of gravity, as his notebooks attest. He believed that earthly gravity extends in an inverse-square proportion all the way to the Moon. Over time, he would edit this theory until his complete theory of gravity was established.

Newton knew there was such a force on Earth called gravity; what he was trying to determine was if that power extended out into the heavens and held the Moon in its orbit. He guessed that this force was also responsible for keeping other planets and moons in their orbits, and called what he had theorized "universal gravitation."

Over time, various trees are claimed to be "the" tree which Newton alluded to. The King's School, Grantham, purchased the tree and had it uprooted and transported to the headmaster's garden some years later. A descendant of the original tree is just outside the main gate of Trinity College, Cambridge, right below the room in which Newton lived while studying there.

So, the apple story is the stuff of legend, after all. Whenever most people think of Isaac Newton, the apple falling on his head is sure to appear in their minds-eye. And according to Albert Einstein, scientists still don't fully understand the force of gravity.

Chapter Four

Work in Mathematics & Optics

"I can calculate the motion of heaven bodies, but not the madness of people."

—Isaac Newton

In 1667, Newton was able to return to Cambridge when the plague epidemic had passed. He was elected as a Fellow of the Royal Society there, and in 1668, Newton acquired his master's degree. He made a commitment that "I will either set Theology as the object of my studies and will take holy orders when the time prescribed by these statutes arrives, or I will resign from the college."

Newton was not particularly religious and up to this point, had not thought much about religion at all. He was appointed Lucasian Professor of Mathematics in 1669, on the recommendation of Isaac Barrow. The Lucasian chair was founded by Henry Lucas in 1663. He was Cambridge University's Member of Parliament. This professorship had been officially established by King Charles II in 1664.

Anyone who had become a Fellow of a college at Cambridge or Oxford was required to take holy orders. This would have made Newton an ordained Anglican priest. The terms of the Lucasian professorship required that the holder actually not be an active member of the church; thereby being able to devote more time to scientific studies. Newton argued that this exemption should hold for him, too.

Since the Reformation, rules that had once been strictly enforced were now disregarded or not enforced. King Charles II was also on the side of Isaac Newton. So, for the time being, a controversy between Church and State, was averted. This was one time where, it seemed, reason won out.

In 1670, when Newton was twenty-seven years old, he began teaching mathematics, now that he held the distinguished chair. In just three years' time Newton aged tremendously; he let his hair grow to shoulder-length, and it became gray, he lost a lot of weight and walked with his shoulders stooped. At thirty years old, he looked like a much older man.

Still, Newton continued to teach and inspire his students. He rarely accepted invitations out and saw virtually no one. He would work late in the evening, and many were the day that he failed to appear outside, taking his meals in and continuing to work on his theories. If he did appear in the dining hall, people soon learned not to try and engage him in conversation; all they would get for their trouble was a scowl.

As well as teaching mathematics, from 1670 to 1672, Newton lectured on optics. During this time he investigated the refraction of light. He would demonstrate with a prism. Prisms at the time were not used as scientific instruments; rather they were looked on as objects of entertainment. The standard against which all other glass was used was Venetian glass. But, these too had their defects.

When light shone through it, it produced multi-colored light on the other side. This multi-colored spectrum presented by the prism could be recomposed into white light by a lens and a second prism.

Scientists such as Descartes, Robert Boyle, John Locke, and Isaac Newton were all leading corpuscularianists. Corpuscularianism is a physical theory that supposes all matter to be composed of minute particles. In the seventeenth century, this theory was important to all noted scientists.

Corpuscularianism was a popular philosophy for centuries and was blended with alchemy. This was the beginnings of chemistry, which hadn't been developed yet, and was concerned with attempts to convert certain base metals into gold.

Newton also showed that multi-colored light does not change its properties by separating out a colored beam and shining it on objects in its view. Newton noted that regardless of how the light was seen—reflected, transmitted, or scattered—it always remained the same color. From this observation, he was able to ascertain that color was the result of objects interacting with already-colored light rather than objects being the source of the color itself.

There were scientists of the time who were adherents of the wave theory of light. They believed that light is made up of waves comprised of white light. They also believed that multi-colored light came from something being wrong in the glass through which it was reflected. Newton, of course, said that light is made up of particles and that the colored spectrum is caused by light as well.

This theory of light was debated by Newton and others including Robert Hooke. It remained a mystery. Yet, from this work, Newton was able to conclude that the lens of any refracting telescope would suffer from the dispersion of light into colors. It wouldn't be until 1676 that Newton revealed the clearest and best prisms to use were the ones manufactured in London, not Italy.

It was in his work with optics that Newton concluded the lens of a refracting telescope would suffer from the dispersion of light into colors. A refracting telescope is a type of optical telescope, one that uses a lens as its objective to form images. They were originally used in spy glasses and astronomical telescopes. Today, the reflecting telescope has mostly replaced it.

To understand the concept Newton was talking about, he constructed a telescope using reflective mirrors instead of a lens. The mirrors were the objective used to form images. This new telescope became the first reflecting telescope ever. In 1668, by grinding his own mirrors, he was able to construct this telescope. It was only about eight inches in length but gave a much clearer and larger image than those used previously.

In 1671, the Royal Society asked for a demonstration of his telescope. Because of the interest from the Royal

Society, Newton published his notes, called On Colors, which later on he would expand into the work *Opticks*.

Robert Hooke, an English natural philosopher, and one of Newton's contemporaries criticized Newton's work. Instead of agreeing to discuss it further, Newton withdrew from any debate concerning his ideas. There were letters passed between the two men in 1679 and 1680. Even with the opening up of correspondence between them, their relationship never blossomed. It would remain poor right up until Hooke's death in 1703.

Newton's theory of light went like this: light is composed of particles or corpuscles which were refracted by accelerating into a denser medium. Thin films had repeated patterns of reflection and transmission. Disposed particles would be reflected or transmitted according to Newton's Theory of Fits. By this, he meant that some particles when encountering an object, would "fit" between the atoms and some would not. Those that didn't "fit" would reflect.

Today's photons and wave-particle duality, all parts of quantum mechanics, are only vaguely related to what Newton believed about the theory of light. In 1675, he published his hypothesis on light, where Newton suggested the existence of the ether to send forces between particles. This idea drew upon the ideas of Aristotle, whose writings were still very much in play at the time of Newton's discoveries. Aristotle's concept of aether, the fifth element, which represented the heavens and space, was used to explain the concept of light.

In 1704, Newton published his *Opticks*, where he explained his theory of light in detail. He considered light to be made up of extremely subtle corpuscles, while ordinary matter was composed of denser corpuscles. This book scrutinized the fundamental nature of light. He explained everything by means of the refraction of light with prisms and lenses, the diffraction of light using closely spaced sheets of glass, and the behavior of color mixtures, with pigment powders.

What *Opticks* did was to set aside Aristotle's theory that pure light is at its basest only white or colorless light. Aristotle also believed that light is changed into color by mixing with the darkness that is caused by interactions with matter. Newton proposed just the opposite: light is composed of spectral hues, all different and all colors. He also stated that color is a sensation within the mind. It is not a property found within the material itself.

Opticks became vastly popular in England and the rest of Europe, and it was read by many. When the book was presented to the Royal Society, it kicked up the debate between Newton and Hooke. Many scientists, particularly in France, still held onto Aristotle's theory of white light; this would go on not only in Newton's lifetime but into the nineteenth century.

One of those in Europe, who was also trying to figure out the theory of light, was a Dutch mathematician named Christiaan Huygens. He argued against the theory that Newton had put out. Newton believed that if light was made up of particles, then the thicker the medium it traveled through, the faster light would go.

Descartes and Huygens believed that light is composed of waves and the speed at which it moved would be slower when passing through denser mediums. None of the experiments that went on in Newton's lifetime, either by him or others, solved the mystery of light's origin. It wouldn't happen for another 150 years.

To Newton's credit, in the end, it did turn out that he was correct; light is both particle and wave, and because of this it stumped scientists for centuries. Scientists in the nineteenth century combined Newton's particle theory with Huygens' wave theory to show that color is the physical manifestation of light's wavelength.

Chapter Five

Middle Years in Scientific Experiments

"To every action there is always opposed an equal reaction."

—Isaac Newton

By 1679 Newton once again returned to his study of gravity and its effects on the orbits of planets. For the most part, he lived a life of solitude, yet it wasn't unpopulated. What crowded into Newton's life were concepts and forms, entirely unknown to others around him. Where people communicated with each other, Newton communicated with his concepts.

Newton referenced Kepler's laws of planetary motion. In 1680 and 1681, Newton's interest in all things astronomical was reawakened by the appearance of a comet in the winter sky. This comet, found by Gottfried Kirch, became known as Newton's Comet because it was the first one to be discovered by telescope.

It was while corresponding with Hooke, who by this time was managing all of the letters for the Royal Society, that Newton worked out what would become Newton's law of universal gravitation. The law states that a particle attracts every other particle in the universe using a force that is directly proportional to the product of their masses and inversely proportional to the square of the distance between their centers. Newton formulated this through inductive reasoning. It is also part of what is known as classical mechanics.

In today's language the law says: every "point mass" (a term used in physics), attracts every single other point mass by a force pointing along the line intersecting both points. The force is proportional to the product of the two masses and inversely proportional to the square of the distance between them. Inverse proportion is a mathematical term which can be contrasted to direct proportionality.

Isaac Newton discovered one of the principal laws of physics with his law of universal gravitation. When Newton observed the apple falling from the tree branch to the ground, he recognized that the force behind it was gravity. The apple's acceleration must be dependent on the mass of the apple. And because the force acting to cause the apple's downward acceleration also causes the earth's upward acceleration, that force must depend upon the mass of the earth as well.

Now, Newton's law of universal gravitation extended that force beyond the earth. Newton didn't discover gravity; his discovery is that gravity is universal. All objects attract each other with a force of gravitational attraction.

As two objects are separated from each other, the force of gravitational attraction between them decreases.

Newton's law of universal gravitation was eventually replaced by Albert Einstein's theory of general relativity, yet it continues to be used as an excellent approximation of the effects of gravity in most situations.

By 1684 Newton sent his findings to Edmond Halley and to the Royal Society in a tract written on about nine sheets of paper. It was copied into the Royal Society's Register Book.

This tract would form the basis of Newton's most famous work of all, his *Principia*. Here is where his laws of motion would astound the world.

Chapter Six

Principia

"If I have seen further than others, it is by standing upon the shoulders of giants."

—Isaac Newton

The years leading up to Newton's publishing of the *Philosophiae Naturalis Principia Mathematica* or *Principia* , as it has come to be known, were productive ones. By 1684 Gottfried Leibnitz, a German philosopher had published his own paper on calculus and from that moment on there was a feud going between Leibnitz and Newton.

Leibnitz wanted to discover how equations could describe the physical world. Newton then claimed he had done this exact work twenty years earlier and that Leibnitz had stolen his ideas. Newton hadn't published his work back then, and it was at this time that he went back to his old notes to prepare them for publication.

Newton had been reluctant to publish his calculus findings because he feared rejection and ridicule from his peers. Yet, challenged by Robert Hooke to prove his theories about planetary orbits, Newton produced a book which would become the foundation for physics as we know it.

During his time at Trinity College, Newton would spend some time at the center court, usually with his colleague Isaac Barrow. He would quietly observe everything going on around him. Even when watching something like a simple game of tennis, his mind was racing off with scientific calculations.

When struck by the racket, for instance, the tennis ball curved in either an upward or a downward direction. He saw that when the ball is hit diagonally, it acquires spin. The side of the ball that is struck by the racket then gains acceleration and motion. Newton had been thinking about just such a concept as this for a long time and seeing it happen before his eyes only brought more proof to his attention.

Newton had the ability to look into the world and see the underpinnings of what made it go. Everyone saw just the scene in front of them; Newton was able to ascertain the framework that held that scene up. He didn't just see a tennis ball being hit from one side of a court to another; he understood the reason it moved in the ways that it did.

Newton lived in a world of ideas, experiments, forms and concepts. It was one of these ideas which gave way to his laws of motion. The *Principia* itself is a work in three books. It deals principally with massive bodies in motion, and Newton did this through hypothetical laws of force and by introducing a variety of conditions. Through observation and by offering criteria on which to decide, he raised many problems of motion.

Newton's first law of motion states that "an object at rest stays at rest and an object in motion stays in motion with the same speed and in the same direction unless acted upon by an unbalanced force."

Suppose you fill a baking dish with water and then walk it around an oval track as fast as you can. You observe that the water spills out of the dish at certain places along the track. In general, the water will spill during three scenarios: when the container was at rest, and you attempted to move it; when the container was in motion, and you tried to stop it; or when the dish was moving in one direction, and you tried to make it go in a different direction.

Water spills whenever the "state of motion" of the container is changed. The water resisted this change in its own state of motion. The water tended to "keep on doing what it was doing." The behavior of the water during the lap around the track is a perfect example of Newton's first law of motion.

Here are some other examples of the law. Trying to get ketchup out of a ketchup bottle. You turn it upside down and thrust it downwards at high speeds, then stop it abruptly. The headrests in vehicles are put there to prevent your head from swinging wildly if you are involved in a rear-end accident. You are riding on a skateboard, and that board suddenly hits a curb or a rock; the board stops, but you get hurled forward, hopefully not too badly injured.

One of the chief concepts brought up with the first law of motion is inertia. Inertia is defined as the resistance of an object to change with respect to its state of motion. Before Newton took it upon himself to study the laws of motion, Galileo had studied inertia, and it applies to Newton's theories.

Even before Galileo, people understood that something was needed, such as push, to keep an object moving. People believed that if you pushed a chair, for instance, the push is responsible for sustaining the speed at which the chair moves. Stop pushing and the chair ceases to move. Galileo looked at this differently. He believed when you stop pushing a chair, the chair continued to go along a certain distance without help from you. He stated that it was friction, or the force resisting the movement, that finally made the chair stop moving.

Newton would build on Galileo's concept of inertia. He said that it was the frictional force that was dependent upon the mass of the objects. All objects resist change in their state of motion; this is because they are all in a state of inertia. It is the mass of an object which determines its tendency to resist change. The greater the mass of an object, the greater its tendency to resist change. Newton also said that the force behind the change in motion must be unbalanced.

Newton's first law of motion also discovered the concept of force. All material bodies have the tendency to stay at rest where they are or move in a straight line. In order for this path to become something else, an external force must be introduced to the surface of the object.

This law was revolutionary thinking. It gave rise to the concepts of gravity and relativity. It is often referred to as the law of inertia.

Because Newton couldn't fit everything into his first book, a second book of *Principia* was planned. Newton's second law of motion has to do with the behavior of objects for which all existing forces are not balanced.

The second law states that "the acceleration of an object is dependent upon two variables – the net force acting upon the object and the mass of the object. The acceleration of an object depends directly upon the net force acting upon the object and inversely upon the mass of the object. As the force acting upon an object is increased, the acceleration of the object is increased, and as the mass of an object is increased, the acceleration is decreased."

This second law can be understood in equation form as $F = MA$. Simply, this is force equals mass times acceleration. In order to calculate the mass or acceleration of an object, simply divide force by mass to calculate its acceleration and divide force by acceleration to calculate its mass.

Some would like to think that these laws and concepts are just for the mathematically inclined or for rocket scientists. But, the second law of motion has many practical implications that you can find in everyday life. Think about pushing a bicycle versus pushing a car. You need more force to be given to the car in order to make it move at an equal acceleration as compared to the force you use to move the bicycle.

If three friends help to push your car, it will be done easier than if you push it alone. The mass remained the same, but the force has been increased by three additional people, which means more acceleration all the way around.

Another example would be trying to kick a rock. You probably won't move it at all, and may even break a toe. But, take a pebble and toss it into the water and watch what happens. The same force is at work here, but it produced lesser acceleration in the case of a heavy mass as compared to a lighter one.

The next time you help out with food shopping, notice how easy it is to push an empty cart as opposed to one filled with food and bags. If you push the cart with the same amount of force, the empty one will go farther than the full one; it just seems to make sense. The full one will be harder to stop. That's Newton's second law working for you.

Chapter Seven

Laws of Motion Continued

"Gravity is a habit that is hard to shake off."

—Terry Pratchett, Small Gods

This chapter brings us to Newton's third law of motion. It states, "for every action, there is an equal and opposite reaction." A force is a push or a pull which acts upon an object as a result of its interaction with another object. What results from these interactions is force. According to Newton, whenever object A interacts with object B they exert forces upon each other.

When you sit down in a chair, your body exerts a downward force onto the chair. The chair exerts an upward force on your body; if it didn't, it would collapse under your weight. These are two forces resulting from one interaction. These two forces are called action and reaction.

Newton's third law proves that there is a pair of forces acting on the two interacting objects. The size of the forces on the first object equals the size of the forces on the second object. The direction of the force on the first object is opposite to the direction of the force on the second object. Forces always show up in pairs; equal and opposite action-reaction force pairs.

Think about when you are traveling in your car on the way to your destination. Cars have wheels that turn and make them go. As the wheels spin, they grip the road and push the road behind the car. Since forces always appear in pairs, the road must also be pushing the wheels forward. The size of the force on the road equals the size of the force on the wheels of the car. The direction of the force on the road (backward) is opposite the direction of the force on the wheels (forward). For every action, there is an equal and opposite reaction. It is the action-reaction force pairs which make it possible for the car to move along the roadway.

A final example is when you're in the car, and a bug hits the windshield. It usually makes quite a mess. The bug hit the car, and the car hit the bug. Which force is greater? They are both equal. For every action, there is an equal reaction. The bug splattering all over only means with its small mass it was less able to withstand the larger acceleration of the windshield coming at it.

What did all of these laws of motion mean to the general population, anyway? It laid the framework to examine everything that is found in existence. Newton's laws of motion helped to create and construct many things. They are used to navigate airplanes, to measure planetary objects in space, to improve one's athletic abilities and to even foresee such things as car crashes.

Newton had drawn on his over twenty years of notes when putting together the *Principia*. The book outlined his own theory of calculus, introduced the three laws of motion and included his account of his theory of universal gravitation. Suddenly, there was a new way to calculate the universe; a way which had never been done or achieved before.

Newton published a manuscript before this one, titled *De Motu Corporum in Gyrum* or "On the motion of bodies in orbit" in 1684. It was from this tract that he laid out his most famous work of all, the *Principia*. Also in this work, Newton made clear his heliocentric view of the solar system.

When Newton's *Principia* appeared in 1687, it was received with the greatest admiration. Mathematicians and astronomers alike were marveling over this great work, as well as philosophers such as Voltaire and John Locke. The educated people of Europe also excitedly welcomed Newton's masterpiece.

And a masterpiece it is. When Newton wrote the *Principia*, he was not contributing to a pre-existing field of study called mathematical physics; he was attempting something altogether different. He was trying to show how philosophers could use various numerical and experimental methods in order to reach conclusions about nature itself; especially about the motions of material bodies.

Principia was Newton's attempt to reorient natural philosophy, taking it in a direction that no one had seen coming. Neither the Aristotelian predecessors nor his Cartesian contemporaries were ready for this. Not everyone was on board with Newton's philosophies initially.

There would be debates to follow, involving John Locke and Richard Bentley and more importantly Leibnitz. He took up the issue with Newton's failure to explain how gravity works. In France where Descartes had reigned supreme, scholars said that Newton's force of gravity had no logical basis and that it was more of a supernatural notion than anything else. In England, the critiques were a little different. His critics worried that Newton's "clockwork cosmos" left little room for divine intervention. Newton believed in God and would continue to believe in God for all of his scientific explorations.

With the success of the *Principia*, Newton began looking beyond Trinity College for new challenges. In 1687, the university sent him along with a delegation to meet with King James II, to protest sending a Benedictine monk to Cambridge for a degree. The king was Catholic, and by 1688, England could take no more of him. In what is known as the Glorious Revolution, he was ousted from power. His daughter Mary and her husband William of Orange were invited to take over the throne. Mary consented only if both she and her husband would be co-rulers. This was the only time in English history that this would occur.

In 1692, Newton represented Cambridge as a Member of Parliament. It was during this period that he also began suffering from insomnia and depression, and for about a year Newton underwent a nervous breakdown. He was so affected by any criticism that he became paranoid; accusing his friends of conspiring against him. He even wrote to John Locke claiming that Locke had "endeavoured to embroil me with woemen."

News of his "Black Year" spread far and wide; Huygens believed that Newton had gone insane. Yet he recovered quickly enough and wrote letters to his friends apologizing for his behavior. Now he lost interest in his scientific undertakings; something else was taking up his time, something more arcane and mystical.

Newton turned his efforts towards alchemy. Alchemists didn't look for proof; rather they sought after those things which are mysterious and other-worldly. It seemed as if they lived in a world beyond reason. Often they were accused of witchcraft.

Chapter Eight

Newton and Alchemy

"The true alchemists do not change lead into gold; they change the world into words."

—William H. Gass

If ever there was a good idea for a medieval mystery, it would surely have involved alchemy. This secretive and mysterious practice is also a very ancient one; one that Isaac Newton spent half his life involved with. Those who knew him said he was on a constant quest for "the philosopher's stone."

This stone is a legendary substance with the ability to turn base metals such as mercury into gold or silver. Because it supposedly had the capacity to extend one's life, it was also called the elixir of life. By converting metals into gold, people believed it would lead them to a greater spiritual life.

By pursuing these practices, Newton was mirroring the times in which he lived. People were obsessed with dying, due to the fact that it was always around them. England had emerged from a tumultuous century, plague still ravaged the land and the fire of 1666 wiped out much of London. The comet seen in 1680 was another sign that the world was soon coming to an end.

By the beginning of the eighteenth century, Newton was hailed as a hero. His writings were well-known, and his *Principia* was known throughout all of Europe. Yet this genius who had worked his way through mathematics and laid the basis for modern physics was also a dabbler in the ancient art of alchemy. Once in his sixties, Newton was practically obsessed with knowing all he could about this magical science.

Presently, Indiana University is cataloging Newton's writings on alchemy; "Yet there is another, more mysterious side to Newton that is imperfectly known, a realm of activity that spanned some thirty years of his life, although he kept it largely hidden from his contemporaries and colleagues. We refer to Newton's involvement in the discipline of alchemy, or as it was often called in seventeenth-century England, 'chymistry.'"

Despite endless experimentation, Newton's alchemical efforts bore little or no fruit. He might have been the last great mind to pursue alchemy, and he initially had great gusto for it; then as his experiments failed he found his interest waning badly. Modern science had yet to emerge; chemistry was alchemy and would be transformed in the coming centuries. It was the lure of magical thinking which drew Newton in, and it would be the failure of his experiments which would be its undoing.

By the beginning of the 1700s, Newton had moved to London and lived with his niece Catherine Barton, who was the mistress of Lord Halifax, a high-ranking government official. Halifax promoted Newton to Master of the Mint. Newton would hold this position for the next twenty-eight years. Newton, with his chemical and metallurgical background, was to come up with new coinage.

By 1703 Newton was elected president of the Royal Society. Moving from a period of discovery to a period of political power, Newton's world was transformed. In 1705 he was knighted by Queen Anne, who was the daughter of William and Mary. This gave him the aristocratic ranking he had always craved. He drew a large monthly salary and employed servants who could take care of his luxurious surroundings.

As president of the Royal Society, Newton actually started stepping out of his imposed self-isolation. He attended every meeting and found he enjoyed interacting with people. The Royal Society was finding themselves in financial straits, and Newton even propped them up with his own finances.

Life was going very well for Isaac Newton. He was indeed a celebrity; crowds loved to gather around him, esteemed colleagues were only too glad to meet with him, artists were eager to paint his portrait, and his genius reputation preceded him. A far cry it was from the yeoman status of his father and mother. Even the Royal Society, which had always seemed an informal gathering of great minds was now brought to heel; they became, under Newton's guidance, a tightly disciplined organization, complete with sound financial backing.

Chapter Nine

Later Life and Death

"To the Master's honor all must turn, each in its track, without a sound, forever tracing Newton's ground."

—Albert Einstein

By 1713, Isaac Newton was a well-known and respected scientist of the age. People were well accustomed to his style of integrating theories and of presenting them with all of their mathematical counterparts. No longer were some of his contemporaries waiting in the wings to tear apart every statement he was making.

It wasn't so very long ago that Newton's theories were scorned by many in the sciences. Now that he was seventy years old, Newton could remember back to the 1670s when so much ridicule was made of theories he presented. Those days were gone.

It was during this year, 1713, that the Royal Society formed a committee to decide, once and for all time, who had invented calculus. The committee found that Newton had beaten Leibnitz by quite a few years. Newton had been made the president of the Royal Society in 1705, and secretly, it had been him who wrote the report.

Leibnitz would not go down without a fight, and he stubbornly refused to give in. In fact, the feud between the two men continued until both were dead. Today it is acknowledged that they developed calculus independently.

By the time he was into his seventies, Newton had remained a quiet giant. For all of his great endeavors, he never boasted of any of them. Always appearing modest, his demeanor was seldom anything but gentle. All of his life he had lived alone, never marrying, never needing the attentions of a woman. As the years went by, he seemed at peace with himself and what he had done.

By the end of his life, Isaac Newton was one of the most famous people in England. He remained the unchallenged hero of all things scientific. He knew enough to invest his great income wisely and regularly made gifts to charity. He lived as the "monk of science" having channeled all of his sexual energy into science.

Toward the end, Newton took up residence at Cranbury Park near Winchester. He remained there until his death. On March 20, 1727, Newton died in his sleep. The Royal Society noted that their next meeting wouldn't take place, due to the death of Isaac Newton.

He was buried with full honors in Westminster Abbey. His funeral was attended by prominent people from all over the globe. His coffin lay at rest in the Jerusalem chamber, a room in the abbot's house in the Abbey. Most of the members of the Royal Society were in his last procession. It was every bit, a funeral fit for a king.

His ornate tomb at Westminster Abbey is inscribed "Mortals rejoice that there has existed so great an ornament of the human race!"

Where once only kings and queens were laid to rest, now this celebrated scientist, whom all of England loved, is among them. Newton was a new kind of hero; one to mark the opening of the door into the modern world. Without him, that door might still have remained locked.

Chapter Ten

Isaac Newton's Legacy

"Could we have entered into the mind of Sir Isaac Newton, and have traced all the steps by which he produced his great works, we might see nothing very extraordinary in the process."

—Joseph Priestley

Newton's fame grew stronger after his death. David Hume, an English philosopher who lived decades later, would say that Newton was "the greatest and rarest genius that ever rose for the adornment and instruction of the species." English poet Alexander Pope encapsulated Newton in one of his poems, "Nature and Nature's laws lay hid in night / God said, Let Newton be! and all was light."

Nothing could have been further from the truth. Newton's achievements were not the burst against the darkness; rather they were one burst, which when combined with so many others opened the door to the Enlightenment and the Modern Age.

Yet Newton's explosion into the world was the biggest and loudest to date. He was the man who never married, never had a lover, had great trouble making friends and fought through his letters with many other scientists over experiments and scientific findings. Through all of this, he had turned his mind to understanding the world in ways which the average person never perceived.

There are a select few who can be credited with the make-up of Western Civilization; Plato, Aristotle, Jesus, and Galileo. Now, Newton could be added to the list. Not every experiment was successful, and there were many days and weeks, months even, when he would be working towards a rightful outcome, only to see it all come to nothing. Then he would begin again. Such was his life.

It seems as if Newton had the magic touch wherever he delved; yet his mathematical systems were not as successful as Leibnitz and his writings on alchemy and other endeavors, never seemed to be his best work. But, those triumphs of which he is so well known were unmatched anywhere. He had no rival. In the science of his time, Newton reigned supreme.

Newton's legacy is more than adding up his discoveries. There were many flaws, mistakes, and his scheming ways to notice; yet all of these changed the direction of science as well. If you visit Gottesman Exhibition Hall at Trinity College, Cambridge, you may run across some old and very faded pages, about who invented the calculus. This debate went on for some time, between Newton and Leibnitz; it had already been decided decades before. Only Newton had never told anyone.

In the 1660s, alone in a farmhouse, steering clear of the plague that was ravaging the countryside, Newton had come up with most of the mathematical formulas that we know as calculus. But he revealed it to no one. In

Germany, at about the same time, Gottfried Leibnitz had also invented calculus, using a different emphasis and a different form of notation. It is Leibnitz's calculus that is used today.

Before Newton penned the famous report for the Royal Society, marking him as the true inventor of calculus, Leibnitz had said, "Taking mathematics from the beginning of the world to the time when Newton lived, what he had done was much the better half."

What he had done was the better half. Nothing that has come since, not relativity, not quantum mechanics or chaos theory or anything, has supplanted that which came from the mind of Isaac Newton.

Conclusion

In the twentieth century, Albert Einstein would overturn the Newtonian understanding of the universe. Time, space, motion and distance, things which Newton had believed were absolute were proved by Einstein to be relative. Einstein was able to show that time together with space are one fabric and that the universe Newton saw was nothing like the universe we know today.

Yet, this would not surprise the great scientist if he were alive today. When an old man and asked for an overview of his achievements Newton merely said, "I do not know what I may appear to the world, but to myself I seem to have been only like a boy playing on the seashore, and diverting myself now and then in finding a smoother pebble or prettier shell than ordinary, while the great ocean of truth lay all undiscovered before me."

In 1936, a metal trunk of Newton's manuscripts arrived at Sotheby's in London to be auctioned off. These random papers and notebooks amounted to 3 million unread words. John Maynard Keynes, a British economist, was horrified to think these would be lost to history and he purchased some of the lots immediately. The rest were scattered around the world.

What Keynes found in these manuscripts was truly amazing: ramblings about ethereal spirits, mercury, a secret fire which covered matter, a fixation on quicksilver, things Newton termed, "the masculine and feminine semens . . . fixed and volatile, the Serpents around the

Caduceus, the Dragons of Flammel." These could almost be names out of a Harry Potter novel.

We now know that Newton did his alchemy experiments hidden behind a pseudonym, Jeova Sanctus Unus. Towards the end of his life, Keynes tried desperately to get people to see Newton not as "the Sage and Monarch of the Age of Reason" but rather as "an intense and flaming spirit."

Isaac Newton changed his world, the one ruled by ghastly experiments, bloodletting, and great superstition. He opened the door that led into our world. He laid the blueprints for the laws of motion and gravity and made it possible for space travel to become a reality. From inventing the reflecting telescope to proposing new theories about light and color, to inventing calculus, to developing three laws of motion and devising the law of universal gravitation—all of these achievements made it possible for modern science to emerge.

Many scientists today would argue that Isaac Newton was the greatest scientist of all. In 2005, a survey was taken of the members of the Royal Society—the same one Newton was head of—asking who had the greater effect on the history of science. Was it Newton or Einstein? The Society answered Newton. The modern world which Newton made possible, still holds him in great esteem.

Made in the USA
Lexington, KY
12 October 2017